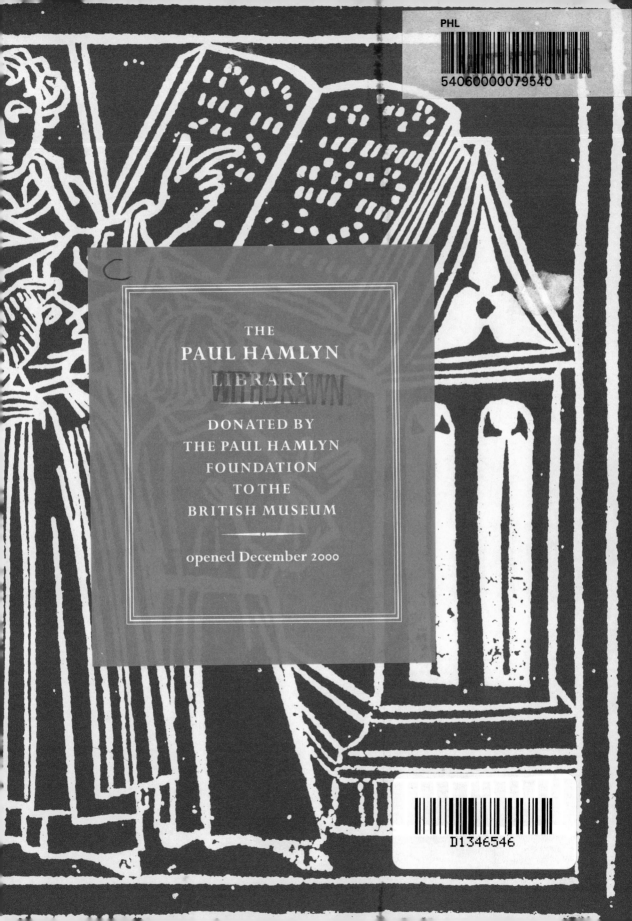

MONASTERIES

R. J. UNSTEAD

ILLUSTRATED BY J. C. B. KNIGHT

A. & C. Black Ltd—London

BLACK'S JUNIOR REFERENCE BOOKS

General Editor: R. J. Unstead

SBN 7136 1043 3

© A. & C. Black Ltd 1970

4, 5 and 6 Soho Square, London W1

First edition 1961
Completely revised and reset 1970
Reprinted 1972

PRINTED IN GREAT BRITAIN
BY BUTLER & TANNER LTD FROME AND LONDON

CONTENTS

*Monks working
as farmers*

ACKNOWLEDGEMENTS

The publishers are indebted to the following for their permission to reproduce photographs:

Aerofilms Ltd, pages 12 (foot), 16, 31, 51; Barnaby's Picture Library, 7, 8, 50 (top); pages 5, 9, 25, 54, 58 (top), the cover photograph and the endpaper are reproduced by courtesy of the Trustees of the British Museum; the Abbot of Buckfast Abbey and Brother Ignatius Birk, 12 (top); J. Allan Cash, 14 (top), 49 (foot), 52 (both); J. P. Dixon, 50 (left); Mary Evans Picture Library, 33; A. F. Kersting, 6, 10 (right), 11, 15 (both photographs), 16 (foot), 28, 44, 45 (right), 57, 64; Mansell Collection 58 (foot); Popperfoto 10 (left), 45; Radio Times Hulton Picture Library, 1, 3, 14 (foot), 17.

Norman font at
Hexham Abbey

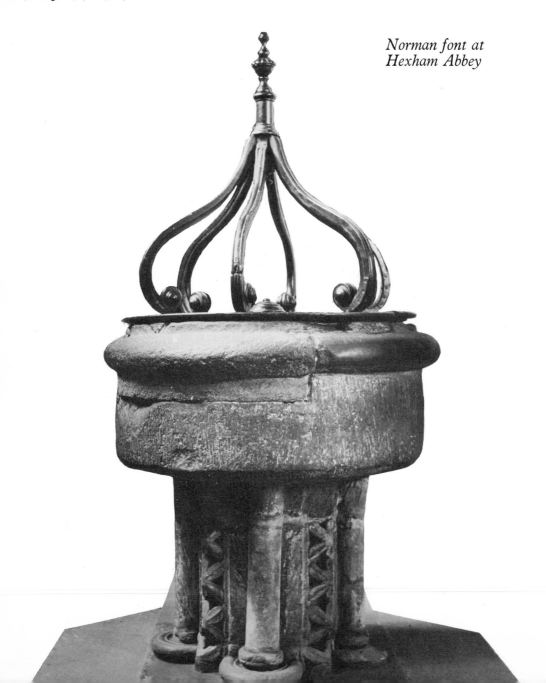

1 THE BEGINNINGS OF MONASTERIES

From the earliest days of Christianity, there were always men who wished to leave the world of everyday affairs to devote themselves to prayer and to the worship of God.

The first monks (the word 'monk' means 'solitary') lived alone in cells or caves in wild or desert places, fasting, praying and scourging themselves. They were called hermits. Monasteries developed when hermits began to give up living alone in order to live together in groups.

Christianity reached Britain during the Roman Occupation, and Saint Alban, our first martyr, was a Roman citizen. Several centuries passed, however, before an abbey was founded at St. Albans.

The Christian faith was carried to Ireland by Saint Patrick. The Irish monks, who went out converting the heathen, lived in separate cells made of earth or stone walls, with thatched roofs. They met together in their little wooden churches and probably at meals.

From Ireland, Saint Columba took Christianity to Scotland where he founded a famous monastery at Iona, which was also a collection of small, separate huts. This kind of monastic life which came originally from Gaul to Ireland and from Ireland to Scotland is called *Celtic monasticism*. It was more severe and hermit-like than the typical life of the monasteries that were about to arise in Western Europe.

The pagan Angles and Saxons drove Christianity out

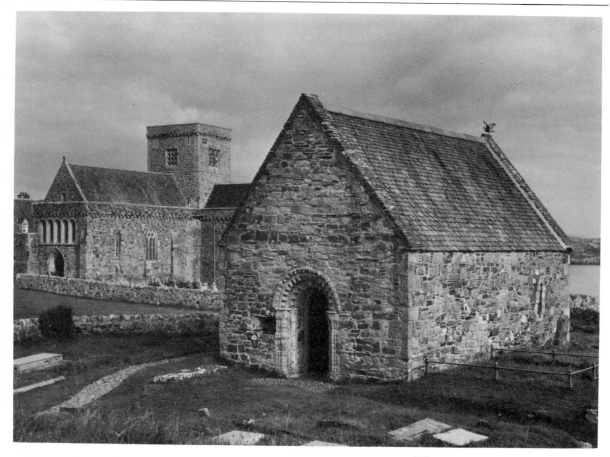

The monastery on Iona today

of England for a time, though it held fast in Wales, where Welsh saints and monks kept the faith alive in little communities, each with a wooden church surrounded by huts made of wattle and reeds. In Wales, many places beginning with 'llan', such as Llanwit Major near Cardiff, Llandudno and Llanbadarn, were once the sites of Celtic monasteries.

2 THE BENEDICTINE ORDER

In the year A.D. 597, Saint Augustine brought Christianity back to southern England and established at Canterbury our first Benedictine monastery, which was different from those which had grown up in the North and in Wales.

Saint Augustine himself was a monk of the monastery of Saint Andrew in Rome which followed the Rule of Saint Benedict.

Saint Benedict of Nursia was an Italian monk who had followed the usual course of living alone in a cave, but he came to believe that this kind of life could not serve God as fully as he wished. So he encouraged some monks to join him in a *community* where they lived a life of prayer, self-discipline, kindliness, and hard work, obeying a set of Rules which he composed.

A Benedictine monk

Saint Augustine in southern England

The ruins of Glastonbury Abbey, one of the earliest English Benedictine monasteries

The modern monastery at Monte Cassino

Saint Benedict, who lived from about A.D. 480 to A.D. 547, founded fourteen of these monasteries in Italy, of which the most famous was, and still is, Monte Cassino, near Naples. His *Rules* were so wise and clear that many more monasteries were built all over Europe. In them, the monks followed Saint Benedict's Rules, and life in each monastery, whether in France, Germany or England, was almost exactly the same. The monasteries were said to belong to the *Benedictine Order*.

In his Rules, Saint Benedict divided the monk's day into three parts. There was, first, the work through the eight daily services in church—this was called the work of God; second, there was work in the cloisters, such as writing, translating and copying manuscripts, reading the Bible, and meditation, that is, thinking about the Word of God; third, there was work in the fields and gardens to provide food and clothing.

The three parts of the monk's day

3 ANGLO-SAXON MONASTERIES

Following Saint Augustine's conversion of south-east England, Benedictine monasteries were established in Kent and Sussex.

In the North, Saint Aidan went from Iona to Lindisfarne, where he founded a monastery of the Celtic type. Others arose at Whitby, Ripon and Melrose.

However, in the seventh century, the Benedictine Rule began to make headway in Northumbria and the monasteries at Jarrow and Wearmouth became widely known.

By the eighth century, Anglo-Saxon monasteries were famous throughout Europe for their learning and art, but the invasions of the heathen Danes brought monastic life to an end, so that King Alfred (who died in A.D. 900) said that he did not know a man in his kingdom who could understand Latin, and his friend Asser declared that 'regular' monastic life had died out.

Later, King Edgar and the great archbishop, Dunstan, brought about a revival, so that over thirty monasteries, mostly in the Fens and the south-west, were founded or re-built between about A.D. 960 and A.D. 1000. They included Glastonbury, Peterborough, Abingdon, Ely, Ramsey, Christ Church, Canterbury, Bury St. Edmunds and Winchester.

Saint Dunstan and Archbishop Oswald of York, who had been monks and who were familiar with monastic ways of life on the Continent, insisted that these revived monasteries should follow the same code of rules.

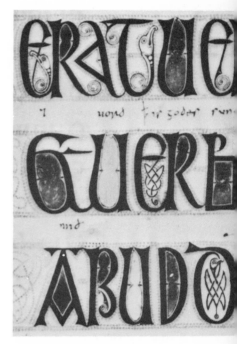

A page from the Lindisfarne Gospel. The text, in Latin, reads 'In principio erat verbum'— In the beginning was the word

4 AFTER THE CONQUEST

When William of Normandy looked round his newly won kingdom of England, two reasons made him decide to reform the old monasteries and to build new ones.

Firstly, he felt that Heaven had favoured his conquest, and, therefore, as a good son of the Church, he must show his gratitude.

Secondly, he despised the Saxon monasteries which had grown somewhat slack since Saint Dunstan's time.

With their energy and passion for building, the Normans had founded many thriving monasteries in Normandy and William was determined to do the same in England. He also intended to make the abbots obey him and serve him as the barons were made to do.

There were, in the year 1066, about thirty-five monasteries and nine nunneries in England, all of them Benedictine, and more than half of them in Wessex; the famous monasteries in the North, St. Hilda's at Whitby and Bede's at Jarrow, still lay in ruins.

William and his friend, Archbishop Lanfranc, brought over abbots, monks and scholars to found new monasteries, to pull down the old ones and replace them by large buildings and cloisters surrounding a vast church.

The abbot directs the masons and labourers

Left and above: Norman church at Iffley, near Oxford

The Norman cathedral at Durham

Stonemasons working at Buckfast Abbey, Devon

From the Conquest to about 1200 was the greatest period of monastic building and influence, when some three hundred monasteries were built and several new Orders came to England. Throughout the Middle Ages, the monasteries continued to play an important part in the life of the country, until between 1536 and 1539 when they were all closed down by Henry VIII and his minister, Thomas Cromwell. During the last hundred years, some new monasteries have been founded, one of the best-known being Buckfast Abbey in Devonshire.

5 BENEDICTINE MONKS

The head of a monastery (or abbey) was the *abbot*, chosen by the monks themselves for his goodness and ability to lead them.

Saint Benedict had said that any one of the monks could be elected abbot, even if he had been born a serf, but he must be a father to the monks, full of good works and of obedience to God. His word was law in the monastery, though he must not give commands that were impossible to carry out.

At Bury St. Edmunds, a new abbot seemed so strict after the old one that the monks almost rebelled, though in the end they confessed their faults, and all was forgiven with tears.

When monasteries were small (and some had no more than a dozen or twenty monks) the abbot lived, worked and slept with the monks as their father. But as the 'house' grew large and wealthy, the abbot became a great man, ruler of many manors, friend of nobles and kings. He was so occupied with a hundred affairs that the monks knew him less, and there were even complaints that it was difficult to speak to him. He had his own house, the *abbot's lodging*, where he entertained important guests at fine dinners cooked in his own kitchen, though he invited certain monks to join him at table from time to time.

The abbot of a Benedictine abbey

The abbot receives a royal guest

Second in command, or leadership, was the *prior*, an important official, especially in a big monastery when the abbot was frequently away on business.

Sometimes the abbey became so large that another 'house' was formed some distance away, even hundreds of miles. This new house came under the rule of the abbot and was called a *priory*, because a prior was sent to take charge of it. The priory remained under the rule of its *mother house* unless it grew big enough to become an independent monastery.

Smaller than a priory was the *cell*; this was a group of only three or four monks who were sent to a distant place to work on an estate and to send its produce and any money back to their own abbey.

Priories and cells were called *dependencies* because they were dependent upon their mother house. Some monasteries had no dependencies at all but others owned priories and cells all over the country. St. Albans Abbey had dependencies in Bedfordshire, Lincolnshire, Norfolk, Essex, Berkshire, Pembrokeshire and two as far away as Northumberland. Monks who were troublesome in one way or another were sometimes sent to these outlying houses.

A large number of cells were owned by foreign monasteries, most of them French. These were called *alien priories*.

In a large monastery, the third official after the abbot and the prior was the *sub-prior* and, beneath him, came all the monks of the house, many of whom had special work to do under the charge of a senior brother.

Fountains Abbey

Monks building their Monastery

The prior

6 MONEY MATTERS

Keeping all the buildings in repair and adding to them was a continual worry to the abbot and the sacristan, for most abbeys were short of money, despite their lands and wealth. One of the greatest monasteries in England was at Bury St. Edmunds, but in the twelfth century it was so deep in debt to money-lenders that Hugh, the gentle old abbot, was literally worried to death, especially as the money-lenders had moved in with their families.

In 1182, the monks of Bury St. Edmunds elected Samson, the sub-sacristan, to be their abbot and he proved so strict and able that in four years all the debts of the monastery were paid and the money-lenders were driven from the gatehouse.

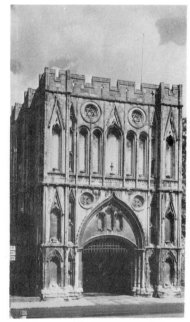

*The gatehouse
at Bury St. Edmunds*

Peterborough Cathedral

The monasteries constantly received gifts from rich men who gave the gifts during their lifetimes or bequeathed them after death. John Paston, for example, left 40s. to his local prior, 6s. 8d. to each of nine monks, but only 1s. 8d. to another, £5 13s. 4d. to the priory itself, and 4d. each for the nuns of Norwich. Besides receiving gifts, abbeys would also look after gold and valuables for rich men who had no safer place to keep them.

The abbot reviews his knights

Norwich Cathedral

It is not always remembered that the abbot, as a lord of the manor, was obliged, like any other lord, to provide armed knights for the king's service. Since he obviously could not send his own people, he had to hire knights, or, later, to pay money for the king to do so. In Henry II's reign the abbot of Peterborough had to provide sixty knights for the king; Bury St. Edmunds provided forty, Westminster fifteen, St. Albans six, and smaller houses, including nunneries, supplied five, three, two or one. If money was paid, the charge was usually two marks (26s. 8d.) for a knight, though much more could be charged.

It is clear that the abbot needed to be a man of business as well as a religious leader.

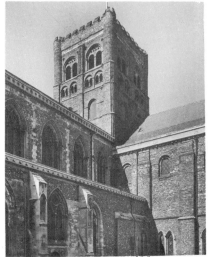

St. Albans Abbey tower

7 THE WORK OF A MONASTERY

A monastery existed to serve God in a number of ways. These were: 1 To worship and glorify God.
2 To help the poor and the sick.
3 To assist travellers.
4 To preserve learning and to teach.
5 To feed and clothe the inhabitants of the monastery in order to carry out the above ideals.

The abbot, helped by the prior and sub-prior, was responsible for seeing that all the work of the monastery was carried out, but he appointed officials (called *obedientiaries*) to take charge of certain duties.

This painting shows Edwin the monk, writing a book. He painted himself at work

8 THE OFFICIALS

The *sacristan* had charge of the church building, the holy vessels of the altar, the valuable linen, the embroidered robes and the banners carried in procession on saints' days. He saw that the church was kept clean and that fresh supplies of hay or rushes were placed on the floor. He also looked after the lighting, buying wax for the best candles, tallow for the ordinary ones and oil for the little stone saucers called *cressets* in which a floating wick provided a light.

Among the duties of his chief helper, the *sub-sacristan*, was the ringing of the bell, which throughout the hours of daylight and darkness called the monks to services. In winter, he was expected to 'supply live coal in iron dishes to warm the hands of those who minister at the altar'.

The sacristan had charge of the church building

You may have heard the word 'infirmary' used to mean a hospital, and this was its meaning in a monastery.

Old and sick monks lived in the infirmary, a separate building in charge of the *infirmarian*. There were beds down each side of a long room, as in a hospital ward, and, to help them to get better, sick monks were allowed to eat 'flesh-meat'.

In the main buildings, the monks were not normally allowed to eat meat, though this meant the meat of animals, since birds were not considered to be flesh. Sometimes a visiting bishop discovered that healthy monks went across to the infirmary dining-room, called the *misericord*, for a meat-meal.

The infirmary

Through constantly nursing the sick, the *infirmarian* and his helpers became skilled in medicine, first-aid and simple operations, so that laymen (that is, ordinary folk of the outside world) came to them for advice and treatment. By this means the monks could earn money to pay for new building. There was a herb garden to provide plants used in making medicines and ointments.

One of the most important works of the monastery was to help the poor, who were very numerous in the Middle Ages when famines and disasters were common happenings. The *almoner* gave away food and clothing, scraps from the kitchen and worn garments, to the poor who queued up daily for their 'dole', or gift. Some religious houses fed an exact number of poor people every day. The meal might be 'a mess of porridge, a farthing loaf and a farthingsworth of beer'; 'porridge' (or pottage) was a dish of beans and peas, with a scrap of meat for the lucky ones.

The almoner must have had a difficult task distributing charity to a clamouring crowd. He had a special duty to look after pilgrims, lepers and beggars, some of whom grew angry if they thought they had not received a fair share. So we find he is instructed to remain calm and 'not to strike or hurt or even abuse or upbraid anyone, always remembering they are made in the image of God'.

The *guest-master*, or *hospitaller*, received and looked after visitors and pilgrims, since there were few inns for travellers. They were given a bed and a meal in the guest-house or in the almonry if they were poor, and were not expected to pay unless they wished to, since the care of travellers was a pious duty. Thus, monks often kept a stretch of road or a causeway (a raised way across a marsh) in repair and even, in lonely places, provided monks to act as guides. Rich guests were entertained with lavish hospitality by the abbot himself in the abbot's lodging.

Receiving the dole

Travellers arriving at the monastery were welcomed by the hospitaller

At Barnwell, a priory near Cambridge, the duties of the hospitaller were clearly set down. 'By shewing cheerful hospitality to guests', he was told, 'the reputation of the monastery is increased . . . God is honoured . . . and a plenteous reward in heaven is promised.' Therefore, he had to make sure that the beds were clean and neat, and there were no spiders' webs in the guest-house nor fires that smoked. When the visitors left, he should be up in time to see them off and to make sure they left nothing behind. He should also take care lest they accidentally took away something belonging to the monastery.

Royal guests sometimes showed little gratitude or thoughtfulness towards their kind-hearted hosts. Edward II visited Peterborough Abbey and cost the abbot a pretty penny; the Duchess of York brought all her household to stay at an abbey in Norfolk and was in no hurry to depart, so that the monks were almost as worried as their brothers at Canterbury who found themselves looking after a pack of hounds for two years after a visit by Edward II's queen! King John is said to have stayed ten days at Bury with all his retinue and to have offered in return thirteen pence and a silk cloth he had already borrowed from the sacristan!

The *cellarer*, as his name suggests, looked after the cellars and storerooms, where food, ale and wines were kept. In fact, he had to attend to everything to do with food, drink and fuel, including transport of goods by land and water, and the buying of carts, ploughs, wood, bacon, salt and dried fish, wine and even clothes!

The cellarer looked after the food and drink, and much more besides

This must have been a tremendous task in days of poor harvests, and slow transport, with a household of anything from twelve to one hundred and fifty to provide for, as well as an even greater number of lay-workers and servants. The manors belonging to Abingdon Abbey in Berkshire provided 27 000 eggs, 1 200 chickens and fifty-four bushels of vegetables a year. As we have seen, monks were forbidden to eat meat, though this was taken to mean the flesh of four-footed animals, which allowed them to enjoy chickens, geese, and birds which we do not eat now-adays, such as doves and swans. Vegetables were less plentiful than today; there were no potatoes, of course. The monks lived chiefly on peas, beans, cabbage, bread, cheese, eggs and fruit with poultry at times and fish from the river or fish-ponds (called 'stews').

There were special dishes of fish and eggs, called 'pittances', which were not very big, but tasty, and these were allowed on feast days and special occasions. Gradually the pittances increased until many monks enjoyed them on Sundays and at least once a week as well. Sometimes these extra rations became so numerous and complicated that a monk called the *pittancer* was appointed to look after them.

The monks sometimes tended to become rather fond of their stomachs and of such luxuries as spices, sugar-loaves, rice, almonds and oranges, which the *cellarer* would buy from the annual fair, making a special journey to do so. At Sandwich, the cellarer of Christ Church, Canterbury, had a warehouse on the Monks' Quay which possessed its own crane for unloading ships, and he was often there seeing to the transport of food and the buying of herrings.

In a big monastery, the cellarer had a *sub-cellarer* to assist him to carry out all these duties.

The Monks' Quay
Sandwich

The *kitchener* drew rations from the cellarer and saw to the cooking, though the actual work was done by servants of the monastery. Sometimes he was a highly skilled chef, for we hear of a visitor to Canterbury being served with sixteen superbly cooked courses, with wines to go with them, in the great abbey where the guest-hall alone was fifty yards long and where, it was said, nearly a thousand persons dined every day.

The monks' dining room was the *refectory* (also called the *frater*) and was in charge of the *refectorian* who saw to the arrangements for serving meals, the table linen and plate. It would be a mistake, however, to imagine that all monks led a luxurious, well-fed life; many of the houses were small and poor; frugal living was observed by many and fasting by all. As a rule, hours went by before the first meal of the day was served, and for much of the year, including winter, this was the *only* meal. Feast-days, as well as the pittances, brought variety and enjoyable extras to the table. Beer was the usual drink, but much wine was imported into England and the monks successfully grew vines in their sheltered gardens.

The refectory. Passages from the Bible were read during meals

Head-shaving in the cloister

The clothes of the monks, boots, shoes, fur-capes, linen and bedding were provided by the *chamberlain*. He also made arrangements for the supply of hot water for feet-washing on Saturdays, head-shaving every three weeks and baths four or five times a year.

Singing and chanting played a great part in the church services, so the care of the music was in the hands of a monk called the *chantor* or *precentor*, who also looked after books.

Saint Benedict had made the care of books an important part of the monk's life and this was perhaps the most precious and lasting gift of the monasteries to the world. Every day in the cloisters, skilled monks, sitting at desks in little alcoves called *carrells*, slowly copied out Psalms, the Gospels, stories and histories on to parchment, using quill pens and black and coloured inks. Often, the pages were illustrated with pictures, and the first letter of the first word on the page was wonderfully drawn and decorated in colours so bright that it was known as 'an illuminated letter'.

A carrell

An illuminated initial from a manuscript

The north side of the cloisters, where the writing was done, was called the *scriptorium* and, at first, books were so few that they could be kept in nearby wall-cupboards, 'certain great *almeries*'. But in time an almery was not enough, and so a special room for books was put in charge of the *librarian* ('liber' is the Latin word for a book).

The *master of the novices* was the monk who saw to the education of young men and boys who were studying to become monks. We still use the word 'novice' for any one who is a beginner. The *novice* went to live at the monastery and, first, had the top of his head shaved bare; this universal sign of the monk was called the *tonsure*. Next, he was given his *habit*, a long robe with wide sleeves and a hood, black for the Benedictines and white for the Cistercians. After preparation and lessons in the cloisters for a year, or more in the case of boys, the novice made his solemn vows of chastity (that is, not to get married) and of obedience to God, to the abbot and to the Rules of the monastery. Then he received the monk's cowl, a very large hood, and became one of the brothers of the *convent*. Nowadays the word 'convent' is used for a nunnery, but its true meaning is a religious community of monks or nuns, or both; the word 'monastery' really refers to the buildings only.

A monk making his vows

In the large monasteries, there might be other lesser officials, such as the *circa*, who was a kind of night-watchman. Duties such as leading the singing in church, serving at table and reading aloud during meal-times were carried out by the monks in turn, each serving for a week at a time.

In Benedictine monasteries, servants were employed to do most of the rougher work, and peasants replaced the monks in the fields. Though the brothers may have tended their gardens and vines, there is little evidence of them doing farmwork after the Conquest. In many cases, lay-workers outnumbered the monks. At Evesham, for example; there were fifty-five monks and sixty-five servants and work people; at Glastonbury in 1189, there were eighty servants and three officials of the abbot's household, whereas there seem to have been only sixty monks. The servants included the porter, gate-keeper, chief baker, cooks, scullions and a swineherd, some of whom held their position for life and handed it on to a son.

9 THE MONASTIC ORDERS

Until about 1100 the only monasteries in England, apart from the early Celtic ones, belonged to the *Benedictine Order*, that is, they all followed the Rule of Saint Benedict; but in the eleventh and twelfth centuries many new monasteries were built and several new Orders were founded.

Scullion   *Swineherd*   *Baker*   *Porter*

Most of these new Orders attempted to return to the strict, simple rules of life which Saint Benedict had laid down, for many of the Benedictine monasteries had become very rich and worldly.

The most important of the new, strict Orders were the *Cistercian Order*, the *Cluniac Order*, the *Orders of Augustinian Canons* and the *Carthusian Order*.

10 THE CISTERCIANS

Some French monks, feeling that their own monastery had become slack, decided to build a new community in a wild, uninhabited place they called *Cîteaux*. Under an English abbot, Stephen Harding of Dorset, and Bernard, a young nobleman, a set of rules was drawn up and in 1098 the great *Cistercian Order* was founded. It came to England in 1128.

The main difference between the Cistercians (White Monks) and the Benedictines was that the Cistercians chose to build, not near towns, but in wild places away from the influence of worldly people.

Cistercian monks building their monastery

Opposite: Norman door at Ely

Thus, their monasteries rose on lonely hills, on bare uplands and in forest clearings. Several were built in Yorkshire, still barren from William the Conqueror's harrying, and in the mountains of Wales.

Secondly, unlike the Benedictines, the White Monks insisted on hard manual work and would accept no gifts except land; they became great farmers and, on the hills, they naturally kept sheep and sold the wool to pay for the building of their churches (since they must not take money presents).

Thirdly, riches and ornaments in the church itself were forbidden, so that there were no vessels of gold and silver, no crucifixes studded with jewels, no gorgeous robes or decorated stonework and carving, as in Benedictine monasteries.

Lastly, the Cistercians refused to employ servants. Since, however, this very strict Order did attract many uneducated working men, the monks were divided into two groups; the choir-monks who attended all the services in church and looked after the business matters and the reading and writing work of the monastery; and the lay-brothers who did most of the farm work and heavy labour. The lay-brothers had a rather different time-table, with more ample meals; and because most of them could not read or write, they had shorter and simpler services in church.

The Cistercians soon had such wide farmlands that some parts were too far off to be worked from the

A lay-brother leading a packhorse

monastery, so little cells (called *granges*), with barns and stables near by, were built. These were looked after by the lay-brothers.

Wool was so valuable in the Middle Ages that the Cistercians gradually became rich without meaning to, and some of their strictness disappeared. Beautiful churches with towers, formerly forbidden, were built, and some servants began to be employed.

The White Monks had seventy-five abbeys and twenty-six nunneries in England, and eleven abbeys and seven nunneries in Scotland. When the monasteries were closed, those in lonely places could not be used for other purposes and so the great buildings fell into ruins. Among the most famous are Fountains Abbey in Yorkshire, Tintern Abbey in Monmouthshire and Melrose Abbey in Roxburghshire.

Fountains Abbey

11 THE CLUNIACS

Another strict Order had been founded in A.D. 910 at *Cluny*, in France, though its influence did not spread widely until Norman times. The Cluniac monks (Black Monks like the Benedictines) gave far more time to church services, so much so that work in fields and gardens was wholly carried out by paid servants, and the monks devoted their days to prayer and chanting in church, and to meditation in the cloisters.

The first Cluniac monastery in England was at Lewes in Sussex, and soon there were others at Pontefract in Yorkshire, and in Norfolk. By 1160 there were thirty-six Cluniac houses in England. Although most were small 'cells' where no more than four or five monks lived very strict and lonely lives, their good influence spread widely. From them men could learn what it meant to live a true monastic life.

The Cluniac monks devoted their days to prayer and worship

The ruins of the priory at Much Wenlock, Shropshire

All the Cluniac houses came under the rule of the abbot at Cluny and all were supposed to send money to the mother house every year. As a result, the monastery at Cluny became very wealthy, while many of the Cluniac houses abroad remained poor. Nearly all were *priories*, not abbeys. Some of the Cluniac houses, however, had magnificent churches, as you can see from the ruins at St. Botolph's Priory in Essex, for the strictness of the Order did not prevent the monks decorating their churches with beautiful sculptures, paintings and stained glass.

St. Botolph's Priory, near Colchester in Essex

12 BLACK CANONS AND WHITE CANONS

The monasteries mentioned so far all followed the Rule of Saint Benedict, though, as we have seen, the Cistercians and Cluniacs lived stricter and somewhat different lives from the brothers in the main Benedictine monasteries.

There were also monks known as *canons*. A *canon* lived in a community like a Benedictine monk, but, originally, he served a large church or cathedral in a town and therefore did more preaching and saw more of the ordinary people of the world than the monk who rarely went outside his monastery.

Since the Benedictines had their fixed written Rule, the canons claimed that they obeyed the Rule of Saint Augustine of Hippo, one of the early fathers of the Christian religion (not to be confused with the Saint Augustine who came to Kent). So they became known as *Augustinian Canons* or *Austin Canons*. Often, they were called *Regular Canons*.

Actually, the Rule of Saint Augustine was not very clear or detailed, so the Augustinians followed a way of life that was very much like the Benedictines, though perhaps with less time spent in church and with less strict rules about fasting and silence.

The *Black Canons*, so called because they wore black cloaks outside the monastery, were popular in England where their first house was founded at Colchester in about 1100. Soon there were wealthy monasteries at Aldgate in London and at Huntingdon with 'daughter houses' in many parts of the country. Two of the best known of these were Merton Priory near London and Bolton Priory in Yorkshire, and the most famous of all was the Priory of Our Lady of Walsingham in Norfolk which became a centre for pilgrims.

King Henry I favoured the Austin Canons and founded a number of their houses. In all, the Augustinian monasteries totalled over 200 in England but many of these were very small and not one had as many as 50 monks.

Some of the Black Canons lived in or alongside an old church in a town but others built a monastery right away from the town and had little to do with the people of the parish. A few of the houses were hospitals, as at the Priory of St. Bartholomew at Smithfield in London and at St. Mary's Priory, Southwark.

A stricter branch of the regular canons arose in France at a place called *Prémontré*. They were therefore

A Black Canon

called *Premonstratensians* or, much easier, *White Canons*.

The White Canons devoted their lives to prayer, manual work and preaching, though, in England, they did not do much preaching and generally built their monasteries in secluded lonely places where, like the Cistercians, they kept sheep and followed a strict set of rules. Altogether, there were thirty-one abbeys of the White Canons and three nunneries.

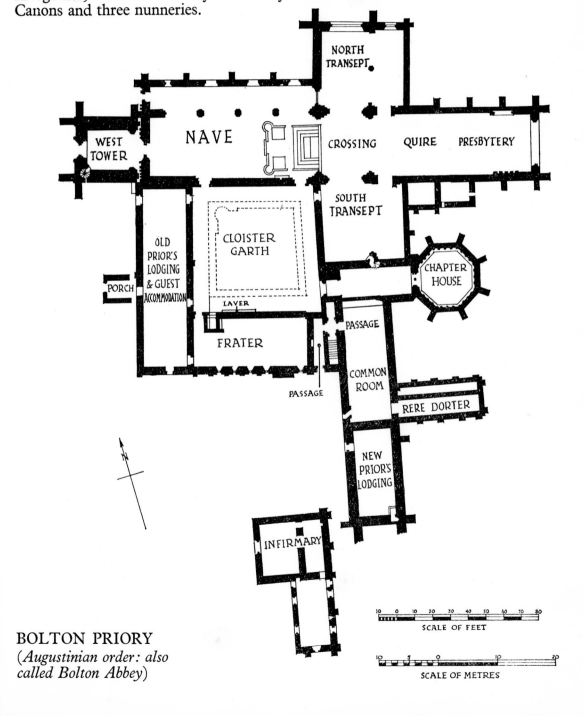

BOLTON PRIORY
(*Augustinian order: also
called Bolton Abbey*)

13 THE CARTHUSIANS

A small but most interesting Order was the Poor Brothers of God of the Chartreuse, known in England as the *Carthusians*, who formed yet another Benedictine Order seeking a hard, pure life.

The first Carthusian monastery was founded by Saint Bruno in a remote valley in a mountainous part of France. Here, in loneliness and silence, the monks could follow a way of life that was deeply respected by medieval people even if only a few were able to endure it.

The Carthusians wanted to return to the earliest kind of monastic life, the life of the hermit. Each monk had his own small cottage or cell, with its study and bedroom, and at the back a little walled garden. His front door led on to a cloister which led to a small plain church. Beside the door was a hatch where a lay-brother could leave food twice a day, which the monk inside took without seeing him or speaking. His day was spent in prayer and reading, with a period for work alone in his garden. His only possessions were his pen, ink, razor, a few books, a needle and thread, a white robe, a black cloak and a hair shirt to irritate his flesh and teach him to bear hardship cheerfully.

A Carthusian monk in his cell

Behind each cell was a little walled garden

The monks did meet each other in church every day at High Mass but they spoke only on rare occasions. Meals were taken in the refectory on Sundays and on certain days of the year; there was a weekly walk and a short period for recreation in the cloister on Sunday afternoon when the prior would allow conversation. Otherwise, strict silence was the rule.

The Order reached England in 1180 when Henry II wishing to make some amends for the murder of Thomas à Becket, invited the Carthusians to settle at Witham in Somerset. In all, only nine Carthusian monasteries were established. These were small and poor, because the monks did not desire wealth or comfort and their way of life was not likely to attract many followers. A Carthusian monastery was built at Mount Grace Priory in Yorkshire where the layout of the buildings can still be traced; Witham in Somerset survived for 350 years and the Charter House in London eventually became Charterhouse School.

Alone of the Orders, the Carthusians never needed to be reformed and they never lost their ideal of a life devoted to prayer and meditation.

Mount Grace Priory

14 NUNS

Although there were over a hundred nunneries in England during the Middle Ages, they never gained the wealth and importance of the great abbeys. Most were small and rather poor, partly because women could not carry out the farmwork, for instance, by which the Cistercians became rich, and partly because nunneries failed to attract rich gifts, though there were wealthy exceptions, such as Romsey Abbey in Hampshire and Barking Abbey in Essex.

Most nunneries were priories, with a prioress in charge, governed by monasteries of the same Order, and more than half were Benedictine. Geoffrey, Abbot of St. Albans, for example, founded a nunnery at Markyate on the old Roman road, a few miles from his abbey, to provide a home for unmarried women from well-to-do homes.

Although the buildings were smaller and simpler, the layout of a nunnery was very like that of a Benedictine or Augustinian monastery. At Lacock Abbey in Wiltshire, for instance, there were cloisters, chapter house, dormitory, refectory or dining-room, the abbess' lodging and guest-rooms.

In some of the nuns' churches, part of the nave was set aside for local people of the parish, though the nuns themselves were screened from view by a partition.

In medieval homes, especially of the nobles, women who failed to find a husband were expected to retire to a nunnery, after they had spent some years as a 'spinster' and probably as teacher of reading to young brothers. Since many of the nuns had therefore 'taken the veil' (the nun's dress) without very much wanting to do so, it is not surprising that there were frequent complaints of their love of fine clothes, jewellery, gossip and pet dogs, which were sometimes taken into church.

The Prioress in Chaucer's *Canterbury Tales* was well-dressed and somewhat over-dainty—

> She had some little dogs which she fed
> on roast meat, milk and cakebread.

A Dominican nun

Apart from church services, the nuns undoubtedly spent much of their time spinning and weaving wool and linen for their own clothes, and embroidering the church garments and tapestries. Since women rarely received as much education as men, they would not have spent long hours reading and writing in cloisters, though it was to nunneries that little boys and girls of good family were sent to learn their letters and first steps in reading.

Chaucer's prioress

Nuns at work

A Benedictine nun

A Servite nun, member of the Servant of Mary order, founded in Italy in 1223 and still in existence

Today, the majority of monasteries are houses of women, and we generally call them *convents*, though, as we have already noted, the word really means a religious community of men or women or both. In the Middle Ages, however, monks outnumbered nuns and held a vastly more important position. Of the 140 nunneries which existed in 1216, very few were as large as the one at Shaftesbury in Dorset which had over 100 sisters and an income of a thousand pounds a year. The nunnery at Barking in Essex was even richer, and there were a few of medium size and wealth, such as Romsey, Buckland and Dartford, the only house of Dominican nuns in England.

Three-quarters of the nunneries, however, were very poor, existing on a few pounds a year. They took lady guests as lodgers and taught children whose parents could afford to pay small sums.

The monasteries themselves, after the Conquest, did not play so large a part in the schooling of boys as is sometimes thought. Most of the novices were being educated to become monks, though a few sons of the wealthy were undoubtedly taught as well. Most boys were taught by their local priest, if he was educated enough, or in one of the schools built outside an abbey or house of canons, and usually supported by the Church with teachers and money.

GILBERTINE DOUBLE-HOUSES

Gilbert of Sempringham, a twelfth century Lincolnshire priest, is the one Englishman who founded a distinct religious Order. He started a convent for seven unmarried ladies of his parish, and this led to the *Gilbertine* 'double-houses' for both men and women. The nuns and the canons had separate cloisters but worshipped together in church, though there was a wall preventing them from seeing each other. Gilbertine houses, twenty-six of them altogether, were ruled by a prioress; the canons were under a prior. A similar Order, the *Bridgettines*, had only one house in England, Syon Abbey in Middlesex.

Later in the Middle Ages, especially in the thirteenth century, a number of different Orders of men and women were founded, who lived in many ways like monks and nuns, but who went out into the world to preach and teach and nurse. Among the most famous of these Orders were the *Franciscans* or *Grey Friars*, founded by Saint Francis, and the *Dominicans*, the *Black Friars*. The *Augustine Friars* and the *Carmelites* (*White Friars*) were similar Orders, which also established a number of houses in England and Wales.

By the time of the Black Death in 1348, the number of religious houses in England was higher than ever before. They numbered over 900, of which nearly 200 were friaries, about 150 were nunneries and some 600 were monasteries.

The number of monks, canons and nuns was greatest in the twelfth century, between about 1150 and 1180. By 1348, some 17 000 persons lived in the various religious houses and, of these, about 3 000 were nuns.

15 THE LAY-OUT OF A MONASTERY

Benedictine monasteries were built to one plan, with slight variations due to the slope of the land or the position of the river.

Canterbury is a notable exception, for there the cloisters are situated *north* of the church instead of south, as was usual. At Worcester and Durham, the dormitories are placed differently from the normal arrangement.

Look at the plan on the opposite page and find the *cloisters* which, with the church, were the centre of the monastery and all that was important in religious life. Round these covered walks, which make an enclosed square, were grouped all the chief buildings. In the cloisters, the monks walked, meditated and worked, and they looked inwards, at a green lawn, and not outwards at the world.

The church itself stood along the *north side* of the cloisters and here, facing the sun, were the carrells for writing and study. Though sheltered to some extent from the wind and protected from rain, it must have been cold work with pen and book in winter, since it was not until late in the life of the monasteries that the arches were closed in with panes of glass.

The cloisters were busy places where monks worked and meditated

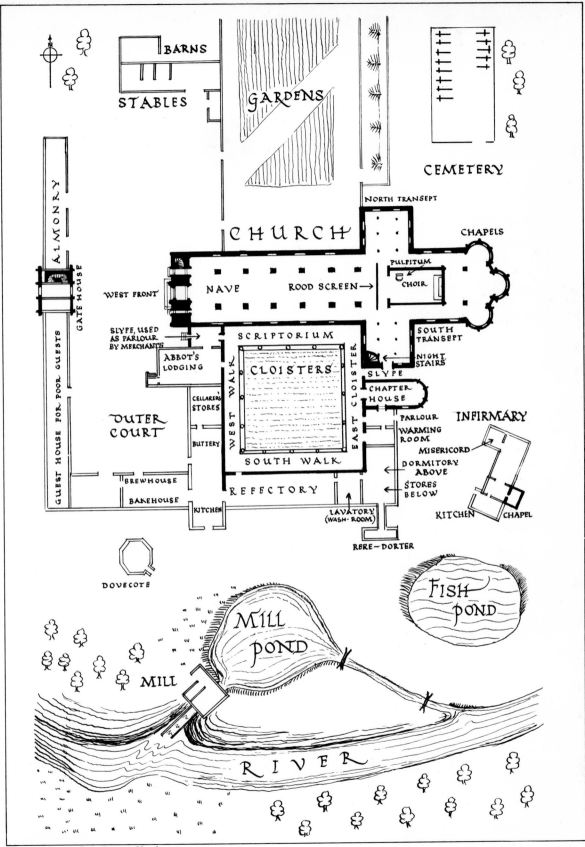

Plan of a Benedictine monastery

Norwich Cathedral—the south door to the cloisters

*Exterior
and interior
of Ely
Cathedral*

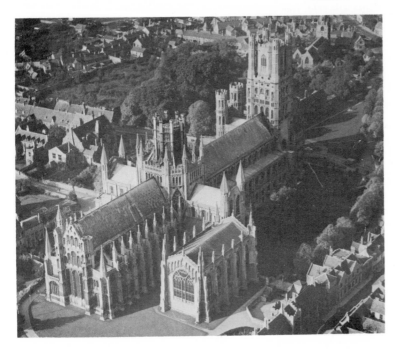

The *east walk* was the busiest, because it led to the 'chapter house' and the refectory, and here, not only did the monks walk up and down occasionally conversing in low tones, but servants and officials came and went during most of the day.

In the *west walk*, the novices might be seen at their lessons, grouped round their master or sitting at their work on the stone benches, though when the master dozed, or was called away, they were known to carve figures on the walls.

At the ends of both the east and the west walks of the cloister were doors leading into the church, and, on saints' days, a slow, colourful procession came through one door, round the cloisters and through the other door into the church again.

The *church* lay north of the cloisters (see page 43). The splendid building towered above the surrounding countryside to the glory of God. The 'great church', as it was called (many of our wonderful cathedrals today were once monastery churches), was different from the parish church, being in fact two churches, one for the monks and one for the lay-people or *laity*.

The abbey church was built in the shape of a cross, lying east-west, with the tower built above the crossing of the shorter arms, called 'transepts'. Sometimes twin towers were built at the western end of the nave, as at Durham and Canterbury.

The upper or eastern part of the church was the *choir*, reserved entirely for the monks. They sat in order of seniority in seats called 'stalls', with canopies above to protect their head from draughts and here they prayed and sang the services every day of the year, sitting in rows

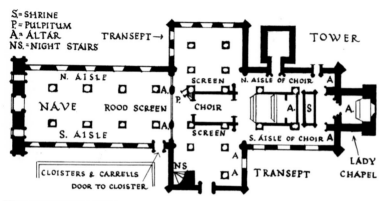

A rood screen

facing each other. The choir was closed in by wooden screens and divided from the nave by a double screen of stone or wood. The first screen, with a door in the middle, was called the *pulpitum*, and the far screen was known as the *rood-screen*, because it bore a crucifix or 'rood', facing down the nave.

The space between the two screens contained stalls for monks too old and infirm to join their brothers in the choir, and overhead was the organ.

Beyond the 'rood-screen' was the long *nave* of the

The nave

church, used by lay-people or, in the case of the Cistercians, by their own lay-brothers only. Thus, the monks and the ordinary people worshipped out of sight of each other, for the monks in the choir did not lead the singing in full view of the congregation, as the choir does today.

On Sundays and on saints' days, a solemn procession made its way through the cloisters and into the nave and to all parts of the church, whose several altars were sprinkled with holy water to the singing of anthems and chanting of responses.

The monks' bedroom was the *dormitory* ('dorter'), situated as near the church as possible, on the east side of the cloisters, above the warming-room and parlour. The first service took place long before dawn, when the monks left their beds and went down the *night-stairs* which led into the south transept close to the choir.

Beneath the dormitory were two rooms reached from the cloister, the *warming-room*, where monks could warm fingers and toes in winter at the only fire-place in the monastery, and the *monks' parlour*.

'Parlour' means a 'talking-room', and here the brothers could meet relatives and callers from the outside world and speak more freely than in the cloisters, where silence was more or less the rule. The visitors entered the parlour by a far door to meet monks coming in from the cloister. A corridor or passage, called a *slype*, often ran under the dormitory to lead to the infirmary.

From the east walk of the cloisters was also the way into the *chapter-house*, a large and lofty room which played an important part in the lives of the monks.

Every morning, after the service called Morrow Mass, the brothers filed into the chapter house for a meeting, which was their parliament and court, presided over by the abbot or prior.

When all were in, a brother read out notices about the services and the saints who were to be remembered; then monks who had misbehaved were asked to confess their faults; punishment, if necessary, would be decided on and this might well be a whipping with the birch. Then the business of the day was introduced to the meeting or 'chapter', and this might include the granting of charters, the purchase of land, the appointment of senior monks

The monks' parlour

A meeting in the chapter house

and officials and the general running of the monastery. Even under the strictest abbot, the monks had the right to give their opinion, and they seem to have voted as we do, by a show of hands. The chanting of a psalm for the dead ended chapter.

Turning into the south walk of the cloisters, opposite the church, we come to the *refectory* ('frater' in Norman

French), or dining-room, where the monks took their one or two meals a day in silence while a junior monk read aloud from a pulpit.

Saint Bernard was shocked on one occasion to find that behaviour in the refectory was not all it should be; 'small talk, laughter and idle words fill the air. Dish after dish is set upon the table and to make up for the lack of meat, a double-helping of fish is provided.'

In the refectory, the prior and senior monks sat at a high table on a dais. The abbot dined in his lodging.

Before and after meals, monks washed their hands in the *lavatory*, which means a 'washing-place'. This was a long room with a raised trough or even with stone or marble basins for washing, supplied with running water and towels, which were kept in a cupboard nearby. Monks were very particular about washing and their monasteries frequently had piped water.

Along the west walk, there were doors leading to the *kitchen*, *bake-house* and *brewhouse*, and also to the *abbot's lodging*, though this might have been rebuilt as a separate house. In that case, the cellarer had his store-rooms here, with the *guest-hall* above.

Beyond these main buildings round the cloisters, and on the east side, were the infirmary buildings—the sick-room itself, the dining-room, where meat-dishes could be served, a second kitchen and a chapel for patients who were too feeble to make their way into church.

The monks' lavatory or washing place

The abbot's kitchen, Glastonbury

All round the monastery was a high wall, with an imposing *gatehouse*, as at St. Albans, which was not pulled down when the rest of the abbey buildings were destroyed because it was big enough to serve as the town jail and also as a school.

Near the gatehouse was the *almonry* where the poor were given doles of food and clothing. Stables, workshops and barns were nearby.

There were several other buildings inside the walls, including the lodging for the novices and a house for the *lay-boarders*. These were people who had perhaps once been fairly well-to-do but were now old and infirm; they had made the monastery a gift of money or land in return for their food and lodging for the rest of their days. This kind of pension was called a *corrody*, and one can imagine how much it must have appealed to old and lonely people, though the abbot sometimes found that the lay-boarders lived too long!

The gatehouse,
St. Albans

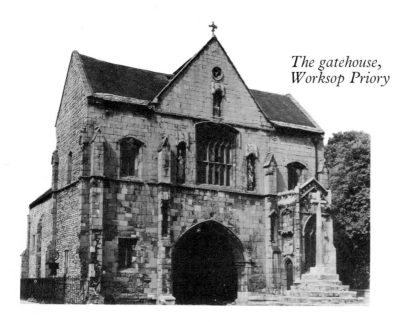

The gatehouse,
Worksop Priory

Fishing in the pond

There was usually a fish-pond and well-stocked river, a mill and a cemetery inside the grounds.

In the reconstruction of Fountains Abbey, you may notice that the arrangement of the buildings is almost the same as a Benedictine monastery, but there are certain differences owing to the Cistercian custom of having both choir-monks and lay-brothers. The west side of the cloisters was used for the lay-brothers' refectory and dormitory. The lay-brothers lived separately from the

Opposite: reconstruction
of Fountains Abbey

choir-monks. To make this extra space, the monks' refectory was built at right-angles to the cloisters, with kitchen and warming-room on either side. The abbot's lodging was at the south-east corner.

The *rere-dorter* was the name for the latrine or, in the modern use of the word, the lavatory. As a rule there was running-water and proper drainage usually in advance of the arrangements in towns.

Fountains Abbey today

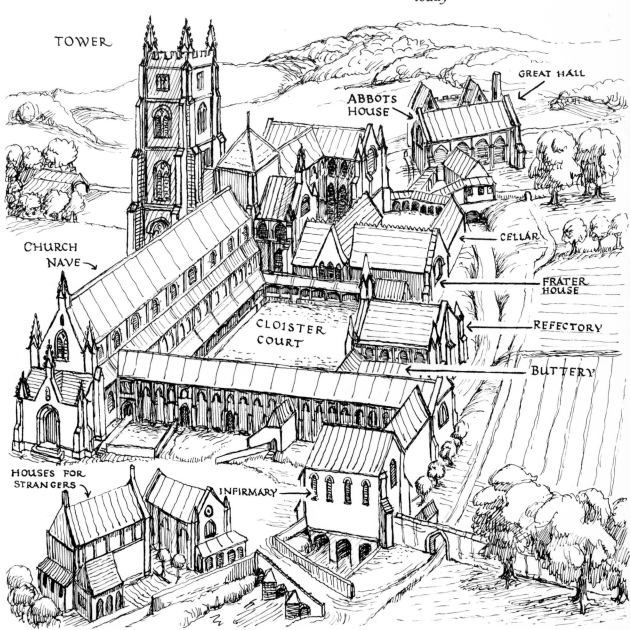

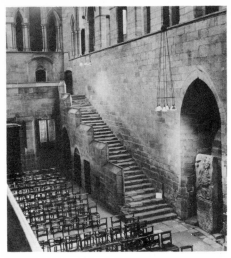

*Night stairs
at Hexham Abbey,
Northumberland*

*Rood screen and
pulpit, Hexham*

16 THE MONK'S DAY

It is not easy to give an exact account of how the monks passed their days because the monastery time-table varied in summer and winter, and also there were differences between the various Orders, and from one century to another. Even if we ignore the Anglo-Saxon period, there were thriving abbeys in England for nearly 500 years, from the Conquest until 1539.

The monk's day began and ended four or five hours earlier than ours. He rose at about 2.0 a.m. and went to bed at about 6.30 p.m. in winter and 8.0 p.m. in the summer. Monks ate fewer meals than we do; it was not meal-times that divided up the day, but the eight services of the church.

Three of these, *Matins*, *Lauds* and *Prime*, generally took place before daybreak; *Tierce*, *Sext* and *None* occurred during the day; the last two, *Vespers* and *Compline*, were at sunset and just before bedtime.

In a Benedictine monastery of the twelfth century, the day might have been as follows: at about 2.0 a.m. the sub-sacristan rang the first bell and the sleepy monks groped their way down the night-stairs from the dormitory, into the choir of the church, which was very cold and dark. By the door sat the *circa*, the monk who noted if anyone had overslept, was absent or late.

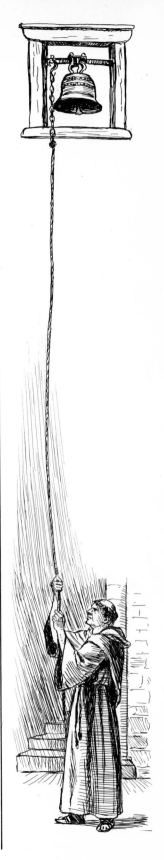

Coming down the night stairs

Singing Matins

Prayers and psalms were sung or recited by heart, in the first service ('office'), called *Matins*. After a short interval came *Lauds*.

Sometimes the monks could now return to their beds until day-break; sometimes they remained in church until the office of *Prime*, held at daylight.

From 7.0 a.m. until 8.0 a.m. was the time for reading and meditation in the cloisters, and then the monks went up the day-stairs into the dormitory to change into day-shoes and to wash, before returning to church.

At this time, or somewhat later, there might be a light breakfast of a piece of bread and a sup of ale, especially for those monks who were excused services in order to do some of the essential business of the day.

The next service was *Tierce*, followed by Mass (Holy Communion) for which lay-people were admitted to the nave of the great church.

At the end of Mass, the Monks made their way into the chapter house. At 9 a.m. when the abbot and all were assembled, the doors were locked, for the chapter was a private meeting at which affairs were discussed which affected every monk.

Lay people used the west door

Chapter ended at about 10 a.m. and then came a brief period of work of various kinds, until noon, when the monks went into church for the service called *Sext*, which was followed by High Mass and *None*, after which everyone was glad to go into the refectory for dinner. Thus, in winter, the first meal of the day was not taken until about 2.0 p.m., though in summer, with daylight coming earlier, it would be at noon.

After dinner, there seems to have crept in the habit of taking a short sleep, but most of the monks would be engaged in work. As servants and peasants employed by the monastery carried out nearly all the manual and farming tasks, the monks occupied themselves with reading, writing, painting and carving; others tended the gardens, fished or looked after the sick. The young monks and novices were allowed to play bowls and skittles.

Evening prayers, called *Vespers*, were said in church at dusk, 4.0 p.m. in winter and about 6.0 p.m. in summer.

Monks playing bowls after dinner

Then came supper, at times no more than a drink of beer in the refectory after night-shoes, which must have been warmer than day-shoes, had been put on. At other times this was a light meal; a monk read from the pulpit.

The last service of the day was *Compline*, and then the monks went to bed. There were rules for getting into bed; monks were to sleep in their shirts, drawers and

gaiters, and to take off their shoes under the bed-clothes! No candle was allowed for reading, and monks were forbidden to sing in bed. Before they slept, the circa would come round with his lantern to make sure that all was well.

A big monastery must have been full of life and interest. Every day, knights, merchants, pedlars, pilgrims and beggars came to the gateway for food and shelter, bringing news of the outside world; wagons and pack-horses brought in stores for the cellarer.

Sometimes the abbot entertained a great noble or the king himself, and then the guest-house was loud with the din of his retainers. At times, the abbot departed to attend the king's council, accompanied by his clerks and a guard, leaving the monastery in the care of his prior. News of the Crusades, of victory over the French, of riots and plague in the town, was whispered in the cloisters and, from time to time, there were crowds of poor villagers at the gate, when the crops failed and another famine threatened the countryside.

There was, too, the ceaseless work of the monastery. It is all too easy to remember tales of fat, lazy monks and to forget that throughout the Middle Ages the monastery was hospital, church, inn, school, library, business house and farm, as well as a centre of religious and civilized life.

All kinds of people came to the monastery for food and shelter

Opposite: the nave of Peterborough Cathedral

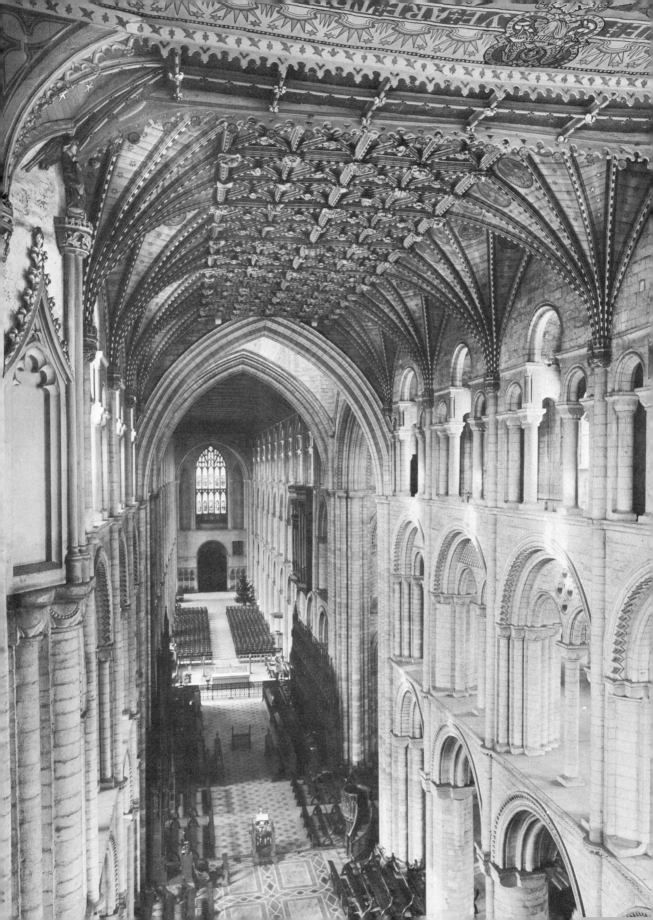

SUMMARIES

1 THE MONASTIC ORDERS IN BRITAIN

ORDER OF SAINT BENEDICT

Benedictines—Black Monks
Cluniacs
Cistercians—White Monks
Carthusians

ORDER OF SAINT AUGUSTINE

Augustinians—White Canons
              Black Canons
Gilbertines—'double-houses'

(In addition, there were Trinitarians and Bonhommes, two Orders which had a few houses in England. Both followed the Rule of St Augustine.)

The principal Orders of friars were the

Dominicans
Franciscans
Carmelites
Augustinians

2 NUMBERS OF RELIGIOUS HOUSES IN ENGLAND AND WALES

Between about A.D. 900 and 1535, i.e. the year before the Dissolution of the Monasteries, the numbers of religious houses founded in England and Wales were:

BENEDICTINES:	Abbeys and priories 163	
	Cluniacs	33
	Cistercians	77
	Carthusians	9 Total 282
AUGUSTINIANS:	Black Canons	185
	White Canons	33
	Gilbertines	26
	Others	14 Total 258
FRIARS:		217
NUNNERIES:		153

Of this grand total of 910, a number had ceased to exist by the year 1535, so, at the time when Henry VIII closed the monasteries, there were between 810 and 820 religious houses in England and Wales.

3 THE CHIEF OFFICIALS OF THE MONASTERY

ABBOT

PRIOR

SUB-PRIOR

SACRISTAN—*looked after the church building and holy vessels*
SUB-SACRISTAN—*worked under the Sacristan*
PRECENTOR (CHANTER)—*looked after music and books*
INFIRMARIAN—*cared for the sick*
ALMONER—*cared for the poor*
HOSPITALLER (GUESTMASTER)—*looked after travellers*
CELLARER—*in charge of food, drink and stores*
KITCHENER—*in charge of cooking arrangements*
REFECTORIAN—*in charge of the dining-room*
PITTANCER—*in charge of the 'extra' dishes (pittances)*
CHAMBERLAIN—*in charge of clothing and bedding*
MASTER OF THE NOVICES—*responsible for the training of novices*

---

4 SOME MONASTERIES IN ENGLAND AND WALES

This is a list of some of the places where there were monasteries. In some of these places, there is still a church or cathedral. Its size and magnificence give you an idea of the scale of the other buildings which have vanished. In other places, there are only ruins.

BENEDICTINE

Berkshire
ABINGDON ABBEY
READING ABBEY

Cambridgeshire
ELY CATHEDRAL
ISLEHAM PRIORY
THORNEY ABBEY

Cheshire
BIRKENHEAD PRIORY
CHESTER ABBEY

Derbyshire
BURTON-ON-TRENT
  ABBEY

Devonshire
ST. NICHOLAS' PRIORY
EXETER PRIORY

Dorset
ABBOTSBURY ABBEY
MILTON ABBAS ABBEY
SHERBORNE ABBEY

Durham
DURHAM CATHEDRAL
FINCHDALE PRIORY
MONKWEARMOUTH
  PRIORY

Essex
ST. JOHN'S ABBEY,
  COLCHESTER
WALDEN ABBEY

Glamorgan
EWENNY PRIORY

Gloucestershire
GLOUCESTER ABBEY
TEWKESBURY ABBEY
WINCHCOMBE ABBEY

Hampshire
WINCHESTER CATHEDRAL

Herefordshire
LEOMINSTER PRIORY

Hertfordshire
ST. ALBANS ABBEY

Kent
CANTERBURY CATHEDRAL
DOVER PRIORY
ROCHESTER CATHEDRAL

Lancashire
UPHOLLAND PRIORY

Lincolnshire
BARDNEY ABBEY
CROWLAND ABBEY

London
WESTMINSTER ABBEY

Middlesex
WESTMINSTER ABBEY

Monmouthshire
ABERGAVENNY PRIORY
CHEPSTOW ABBEY
USK PRIORY

Norfolk
NORWICH CATHEDRAL
WYMONDHAM PRIORY

Northamptonshire
PETERBOROUGH ABBEY

Northumberland
LINDISFARNE PRIORY
TYNEMOUTH PRIORY

Nottinghamshire
BLYTH PRIORY

Oxford
EYNSHAM ABBEY

Shropshire
SHREWSBURY ABBEY

Somerset
ATHELNEY ABBEY
BATH ABBEY
GLASTONBURY ABBEY
MUCHELNEY ABBEY

Staffordshire
SANDWELL PRIORY

Suffolk
BURY ST. EDMUNDS
ABBEY

Surrey
CHERTSEY ABBEY

Sussex
BATTLE ABBEY
BOXGROVE PRIORY

Warwickshire
ALCESTER ABBEY
COVENTRY ABBEY

Wiltshire
MALMESBURY ABBEY

Worcestershire
EVESHAM ABBEY
MALVERN ABBEY
PERSHORE ABBEY
WORCESTER CATHEDRAL

Yorkshire
SELBY ABBEY
WHITBY ABBEY
ST. MARY'S ABBEY,
YORK
HOLY TRINITY PRIORY,
YORK

CLUNIAC

Devon
BARNSTAPLE

Essex
ST. BOTOLPH'S PRIORY,
COLCHESTER

Norfolk
CASTLE ACRE, THETFORD

Northamptonshire
DAVENTRY

Nottinghamshire
LENTON

Surrey
BERMONDSEY

Sussex
LEWES

Somerset
MONTACUTE

Shropshire
WENLOCK

Yorkshire
PONTEFRACT

CISTERCIAN

Caernarvonshire
CONWAY ABBEY

Cumberland
CALDER ABBEY
HOLME CULTRAM ABBEY

Denbighshire
VALLE CRUCIS ABBEY

Dorset
BINDON ABBEY
FORDE ABBEY

Essex
TILTY ABBEY

Flintshire
BASINGWERK ABBEY

Glamorgan
MARGAM ABBEY
NEATH ABBEY

Gloucestershire
HAILES ABBEY
KINGSWOOD ABBEY

Hampshire
BEAULIEU ABBEY
NETLEY ABBEY

Herefordshire
DORE ABBEY

Lancashire
FURNESS ABBEY
WHALLEY ABBEY

Lincolnshire
KIRKSTEAD ABBEY

Merioneth
CYMMER ABBEY

Monmouthshire
TINTERN ABBEY

Northumberland
HEXHAM PRIORY
NEWMINSTER ABBEY

Nottinghamshire
RUFFORD ABBEY

Oxfordshire
THAME ABBEY

Pembrokeshire
HAVERFORDWEST PRIORY

Shropshire
BUILDWAS ABBEY

Staffordshire
CROXDEN ABBEY

Surrey
WAVERLEY ABBEY

Warwickshire
MEREVALE ABBEY

Yorkshire
RIEVAULX ABBEY
WALTON PRIORY
BYLAND ABBEY
FOUNTAINS ABBEY
JERVAULX ABBEY
KIRKSTALL ABBEY

AUGUSTINIAN BLACK CANONS

Anglesey
PENMON PRIORY

Cornwall
DUNSTABLE PRIORY
ST. GERMAN'S PRIORY

Cumberland
CARLISLE CATHEDRAL
LANERCOST PRIORY

Essex
COLCHESTER PRIORY
ST. OSYTH'S ABBEY
WALTHAM ABBEY

Gloucestershire	London	Nottinghamshire	Suffolk
BRISTOL ABBEY	ST. BARTHOLOMEW'S, SMITHFIELD	WORKSOP PRIORY NEWSTEAD PRIORY	HEMINGFLEET PRIORY
Hampshire	SOUTHWARK CATHEDRAL		*Warwickshire*
CHRISTCHURCH PRIORY PORTCHESTER PRIORY	*Monmouthshire*	*Oxfordshire*	MAXSTOKE PRIORY
	LLANTHONY PRIORY	OXFORD CATHEDRAL ST. FRIDESWIDE'S PRIORY	*Yorkshire*
Lancashire	*Norfolk*		BOLTON PRIORY
CARTMEL PRIORY	CREAKE ABBEY WALSINGHAM PRIORY	*Shropshire*	BRIDLINGTON PRIORY GUISBOROUGH PRIORY
Lincolnshire		HAUGHMOND PRIORY LILLESHALL PRIORY	KIRKHAM PRIORY
BOURN PRIORY THORNTON ABBEY	*Northumberland*		
	BRINKBURN PRIORY		

AUGUSTINIAN WHITE CANONS (PREMONSTRATENSIANS)

Carmarthenshire	Lancashire	Suffolk	Westmorland
TALLEY ABBEY	COCKERSAND ABBEY	LEISTON ABBEY	SHAP ABBEY
Devonshire	*Northumberland*	*Sussex*	*Yorkshire*
TORRE ABBEY	ALNWICK ABBEY BLANCHARD ABBEY	BAYHAM ABBEY	COVERHAM ABBEY EASBY ABBEY
Hampshire			EGGLESTONE ABBEY
TITCHFIELD ABBEY			

CARTHUSIAN

Somerset	London	Yorkshire
HINTON CHARTERHOUSE WITHAM CHARTERHOUSE	LONDON CHARTERHOUSE	MOUNT GRACE PRIORY

GILBERTINE

Nottinghamshire	Yorkshire
MATTERSEY PRIORY	MALTON PRIORY WATTON PRIORY

5 SOME NUNNERIES IN ENGLAND

BENEDICTINE

Dorset
SHAFTESBURY ABBEY

Hampshire
ROMSEY ABBEY

Hertfordshire
SOPWELL

Kent
SHEPPEY MINSTER

Yorkshire
MANICK PRIORY

NUN MONKTON PRIORY
NUNBEELING PRIORY
THICKET PRIORY
WILBERFOSS PRIORY

AUGUSTINIAN

Shropshire
WHITE LADIES PRIORY

Wiltshire
LACOCK ABBEY

BRIDGETTINE

Middlesex
SYON ABBEY

FRANCISCAN

Cambridgeshire
DENNEY ABBEY

CISTERCIAN

Yorkshire
BAYSDALE PRIORY
HANDALE PRIORY
KIRKLEES PRIORY
WYKEHAM PRIORY
YEDINGHAM PRIORY

6 MONASTERIES IN SCOTLAND

In Scotland, the Celtic monasteries, consisting of a few hermits' huts grouped round a small church, had mostly disappeared by the end of the seventh century, and no Benedictine houses were established in Saxon times as they were in England.

It was not until about 1074 that Queen Margaret, wife of Malcolm Canmore, founded Dunfermline Abbey, the first and the only large Benedictine monastery in Scotland. Margaret's sons, Edgar, Alexander I and David I, continued her work. Half English by birth and upbringing, they turned to England and the continent for help in planting monasticism on Scottish soil. Between them, they invited the Cluniacs, Augustinians, Cistercians, Premonstratensians and others to establish houses in the country.

David I also introduced an Order almost unknown in England, the *Tironensians* (from Tiron in Brittany). This Order was an offshoot of Cluny, but the monks lived more like Cistercians, favouring handicrafts rather than sheep-raising. Another unusual Order was the *Valliscaulian* Order from Burgundy, which had three priories in remote parts of the north and the west. Its monks lived even stricter lives than the Carthusians, who had just one priory, at Perth.

Whereas in England, Cluniac houses were nearly always priories, both those in Scotland were abbeys. The Cistercians, renowned for their lives in lonely places, built at least eleven abbeys, yet they made little or no attempt to penetrate the Highlands.

The four Orders of friars—Franciscan, Carmelite, Dominican and Augustinian—all established friaries in Scotland, and there were also the *Trinitarians*, an Order of canons, sometimes called the 'red friars'. Nunneries, however, were few, probably not more than fifteen, and most were very poor and small, for we read of only one with as many as thirty nuns and others with a prioress and two, five or six nuns.

Melrose, Jedburgh and Dryburgh were splendid abbeys, but, generally speaking, Scottish monasteries were smaller and less wealthy than in England. Most were situated in central and southern Scotland, but in the remote regions of the north and the west there was scarcely one.

Henry VIII closed the English monasteries in 1536 to 1539, but his rule did not extend to Scotland. There, they lingered on for up to another fifty years; some were sacked by English troops, some by lawless mobs who were particularly severe on the friaries in towns, while others were gradually taken over by lords and by the Crown.

The ruins of Melrose Abbey, built by David I, with the help of monks from Rievaulx Abbey, Yorkshire

Here is a short list of Scottish monasteries:

BENEDICTINE (2): Dunfermline Abbey, Coldingham Priory

CLUNIAC (2): Crossraguel Abbey, Paisley Abbey

TIRONENSIAN (4 abbeys): Arbroath, Kelso, Kilwinning, Lindores

CISTERCIAN (11 abbeys): Balmerino, Coupar Angus, Culross, Deer, Dundrennan, Glenluce, Kinloss, Melrose, Newbattle, Saddell, Sweetheart

PREMONSTRATENSIAN (2): Dryburgh Abbey, Whithorn Priory

VALLISCAULIAN (3 priories): Ardchattan, Beauly, Pluscarden

AUGUSTINIAN (7): Cambuskenneth Abbey, Holyrood Abbey, Jedburgh Abbey, Inchcolm Priory, Inchmahome Priory, Restenneth Priory, St Andrews Priory

TRINITARIAN (8 houses): Aberdeen, Berwick, Dirleton, Dunbar, Fail, Houston, Peebles, Scotlandwell

CARTHUSIAN (1): Perth

GILBERTINE (1): Dalmilling

Sweetheart Abbey, Kirkcudbrightshire